SOUSED
AT THE
MANOR

SOUSED

AT THE

MANOR

SOUSED

AT THE

MANOR

An Invitation to Classic Risque Cocktails
with a Modern Twist

BRIAN CRAWFORD

atmosphere press

Cocktail Concoctions

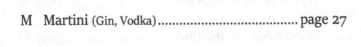

A cocktail guide for you to imbibe.
You'll tell all your friends,
You'll show them with pride.
And this they'll agree,
None will deny,
They won't put it down,
Until all have been tried!

Soon you will see,
In this I don't lie,
A fun time by all
Awaits you inside.

A is for Anisette,
Which I drink with Antoinette.
She's a woozy as a floozy,
And I'll prove it on a bet.

Marie Anisette

1 oz anisette
1/2 oz cognac
1/2 oz whipping cream
1/2 oz egg
Freshly grated nutmeg
Fresh orange zest

Dry shake ingredients, then shake with ice. Strain into Nick and Nora glass. Garnish with fresh grated nutmeg and orange zest.

"Let them drink cake."

Brandy, Brandy,
"Her lips are like candy," said the men eyeing Sandy.

Although she prefer they have more candor,
she may let them have a gander,
After a little more Brandy Alexander.

Brandy Alexander the Great ◆—

1 oz bottled-in-bond brandy
½ oz dark crème de cacao
½ oz hazelnut liqueur
1 scoop vanilla ice cream
½ tsp instant espresso

Stir brandy, hazelnut liqueur and creme de cacao to combine, pour over scoop of vanilla ice cream in coup glass. Dust with espresso powder to garnish.

"I have nothing to do each day,
but write, drink, and run out of money."

- Robert Black

Mrs. Fontaine adored Champagne.
It appeared to be her bane.

Although Liquor may be quicker,
Champagne was her elixir,
Which she guzzled down in vain

Champagne Supernova

1 oz gin
1/2 oz Elderflower liqueur
1/2 oz Aperol
1/2 oz lemon juice
2 dashes orange bitters
Top with champagne
Orange twist

Shake spirits, bitters and juices to combine. Strain into a coupe and top with champagne. Express orange twist and dispose of it.

"There comes a time in every woman's life when the only thing that helps is a glass of champagne."

- Bette Davis

"You are simply **D**ivine!"
Said Susie to her friend Zachary.
"Show me yours, and I'll show you mine,"
He suggested and patted her behind.
And although he doesn't have a dime,
Susie may, with time.
For if there is one thing about his flattery,
It sounds better with every drop of raspberry.

◆ Divine Wind ◆

2 oz gin (or vodka)
3/4 oz dry curacao
1/2 oz raspberry liqueur
1/2 oz lime juice
1/4 oz simple syrup
Orange twist

Combine all liquid ingredients except raspberry liqueur over ice into a shaker. Shake and strain into a martini glass. Slowly sink raspberry liqueur into the glass, express and discard orange twist.

"I like to have a martini,
Two at the very most.
After three I'm under the table,
After four I'm under my host."

- Dorothy Parker, *The Collected Dorothy Parker*

E is for **E**lixir,
That dangerous wonderful mixer.

As Ron continued to party,
Laughing loud and all fool hardy,

Mary whispered, "I'll be down by the gate,"
Knowing Ron would take the bait.

Kate chuckled to her friend Larry,
Knowing full well that Mary was Harry!

◆— Elixir of Immortality —◆

2 oz bottled-in-bond bourbon

Pour ingredients into rocks glass.

"You chose... wisely."

"This is turning into an
alcohol-will-cure-everything kind of day."

- Kelly Moran, *Bewitched*

"I just made a "**F**reudian Slip,'"
Sandra said with a wink and a quip.

Francis said, "You are way too cool.
Care to meet me at the pool?"

Sandra replied as she revealed her slip,
"Only if we skinny dip!"

◈ Freudian Sip ◈

3/4 oz gin
3/4 oz licor 43
3/4 oz chartreuse
3/4 oz fernet
3/4 oz lime juice
1/4 oz simple syrup
Lemon twist

Shake ingredients and strain into cocktail glass. Express and discard lemon twist.

"It provokes the desire, but takes away the performance."

- William Shakespeare, *Macbeth*

"Gin, gin...to spill is a sin!"
Roxy said to Butler Jim.
"To sip is divine, but bide your time,
For gin after gin,
Will make the room spin."

◆ Jealousy ◆

1 1/2 oz gin
3/4 oz limoncello
3/4 oz raspberry liqueur
1/2 oz lemon juice
Egg white
Fresh basil
Lemon twist

Dry shake all wet ingredients together. Slap basil and add to shaker, along with ice. Shake, strain through mesh strainer into coupe. Express and discard lemon twist, garnish with one full basil leaf.

"If you don't expect too much from me,
you might not be let down."

-Gin Blossoms

Thomas Trim said to Samantha Frowel,
"I love this party, why the scowl?"

"Life is a ball but not for all,
I hate this party, a car I called!"

With that she turned and stormed down the hall.

"That's absurd!" Tom said to his **H**ighball.

Highball

2 oz liquor
Carbonated mixer of choice

Pour liquor over ice into high ball glass. Top with carbonated mixer of choice. Garnish, or don't. Limes are usually a safe bet.

"Everything should be made
as simple as possible, but not simpler."

- Albert Einstein

"A kiss, a kiss, is all that I wish,"
Jack Scott said to Miss Mariss.

"Although I'm sure you would adore,
You're not my type, to me you're a bore."

Leaving Jack embarrassed and pissed,
He drowned his anger in an Irish Whiskey
with a twist.

◆ Irish Goodbye ◆

2 oz Irish whiskey
1/2 oz ginger liqueur
1/2 oz limoncello
1/2 oz Drambuie
2 dashes Angostura bitters, Lemon twist

Combine liquor and bitters over ice and stir. Strain into a rocks glass with one large cube. Express and discard the lemon twist.

"What whiskey will not cure, there is no cure for."

- Irish Proverb

"**J**uice is still better than rye or goose!"
Juliet exclaimed to Peter Pruce.

"Although it may be time to call a truce,
For one more juice may be my noose."

◆ Juice Box ◆

1 oz spiced rum
1 oz dark rum
1/2 oz dry curaçao
1/2 oz Cherry Heering
1/2 oz amaretto
2 oz pineapple juice

3/4 oz lime juice
1/4 oz simple syrup
2 dashes angostura bitters
Orange wheel
Cherry

Pour all ingredients into a strainer with ice. Shake and pour into a highball glass. Garnish with orange wheel and cherry.

"Oh so you hate your job? Why didn't you say so?
There's a support group for that. It's called EVERYBODY,
and they meet at the bar."

- Drew Carey

"A tiger he becomes with each **K**amikaze.
I would never let him maul and paw me!"

Sally spoke softly, "It may seem cruel,
But it's a small price to pay for diamonds and jewels."

Kamikaze Radioactive

Pour into a cocktail shaker with ice:

½ oz. Light Rum
½ oz. Coconut Rum
½ oz. 151 Rum
½ Blue Curacao
1 oz. Fresh Lime Juice
½ oz. Grenadine

Stir and strain into a cocktail glass and garnish with a pineapple wedge.

Death: "There are better things in life than alcohol, Albert."
Albert: "Oh, yes, sir. But alcohol sort of compensates
for not getting them."

- Terry Pratchett

Kamikaze Radioactive

"I adore my iced tea from the Island of Long, The
gin the tequila and the vodka so strong!"

She proclaimed in prose,
Her voice like a song,
A gleam in her eye,
Her hair shinny blonde.

"She's fun," Bob said to the gentleman Thom.
"She is," Thom said, as he reached for the tongs,
"But not quite as fun while her clothes are still on."

Literally Anywhere Not Long Island

2 oz (black tea infused) bourbon
1/2 oz limoncello
1/2 oz Pimm's
1/2 oz lemon juice

1/4 oz simple syrup
2 dashes angostura bitters
Ginger beer
Lemon wedge

Shake liquors, juice, bitters and syrup with ice. Strain over ice into highball glass. Top with ginger beer. Garnish with lemon wedge.

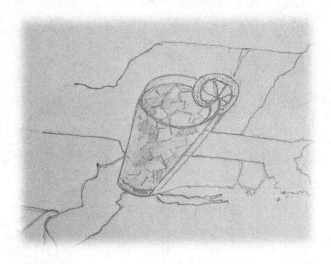

Long Island is not mentioned in "Empire State of Mind," "New York State of Mind," or "New York, New York."

There is a reason for this.

Oh the **M**artini
So sophisticated and seemly.
Roger had four,
Told his boss he's a boor.
Though Roger has learned Martinis speak freely,
He's soon to learn unemployment pays teeny.

3 oz gin (or vodka)
1/2 oz dry vermouth
Lemon twist or Olive

Combine gin and vermouth over ice, stir. Strain into a martini glass. Express and discard lemon twist or add olive.

"I had never tasted anything so cool and clean.
They made me feel civilized."

- Hemingway, *A Farewell to Arms*

Betty Hall was the belle of the ball,
Leaving with men both short and tall.

Although perhaps just a slanderous attack,
They say Betty is a **N**ymphomaniac,
Who entertains men,
In the back of her Cadillac.

Nymphomaniac

2 oz coconut rum
1/2 oz Midori
1/2 oz Licor 43
1 1/2 oz pineapple juice
1/2 oz lime juice
1/2 oz vanilla simple syrup
Cucumber
Balled melon (cantaloupe and/or honeydew)

Muddle cucumber in shaker, pour in liquors, juices and syrup. Add ice, shake and strain with a mesh filter into coupe glass. Garnish with three skewered melon balls.

"I don't know the question, but sex is definitely the answer."

- Woody Allen

"Old Fashioned, my dear,"
Said Mrs. Jane Patton.

The Bartender winked and admired her passion.
"Your eyes and your smile are simply dashin'"
The Bartender smiled in complete satisfaction.

⟶◆ Old Fashioned ◆⟵

3 oz bottled in bond bourbon (or bonded rye)
1 demerara sugar cube
2 dashes angostura bitters
2 dashes orange bitters
Orange twist

Place sugar cube in empty rocks glass. Add angostura and orange bitters, muddle sugar cube with the bitters to form a slurry. Add one large ice cube. Pour whiskey over ice cube. Express orange twist, discard if desired.

"I like my whiskey old and my women young."

- Errol Flynn

"The **P**ope is on vacation in this destination,"
Plump Perry said to his congregation.

"Drink and be merry.
In this we can't fail,
for tomorrow will come,
And to Mary we'll hail!"

Pope's Amnesty

2 oz vanilla infused white rum
1 oz bianco vermouth
3/4 oz lime juice
1/4 oz rich gomme syrup
1 dash Peychaud's bitters

Pour liquors and juice over ice into a shaker, shake. Strain into coup glass. Add one violent dash of Peychaud's bitters to garnish.

Fell in love with a beautiful blonde once. Drove me to drink.
And I never had the decency to thank her."

- W.C. Fields

"I'll give you a penny for a peck,"
Sailor Sam said to Miss Fleck.

"You're as bold as I've been told.
Meet me on the **Q**uarterdeck."

◆ Quarterdeck ◆

2 oz black rum
1 oz Lustau East India Solera Sherry
1/2 oz Cynar
1/2 oz lime juice
2 dashes Angostura bitters Sea salt
Orange twist

Combine liquor, juice and bitters into a shaker with ice, shake and strain into a coupe glass half-rimmed with sea salt. Express and discard orange twist.

"Any damn fool can navigate the world sober.
It takes a really good sailor to do it drunk."

- Sir Francis Chich

Rita became increasingly dumb
With each passing runner of **R**um.

She may not know her finger from thumb,
Though she couldn't be accused of not knowing fun.

➤◆ Rum Runner ◆➤

1 oz coconut rum
1 oz spiced rum
1 oz black rum
1/2 oz creme de banane
1 oz pineapple juice

1 oz orange juice
1/2 oz lime juice
1/2 oz grenadine
Pineapple wedge
Cherry

Combine liquors and juices over ice into a shaker. Shake and strain over ice into highball glass. Add grenadine into glass. Garnish with skewered pineapple and cherry.

"It was a maddening image and the only way to whip it was to hang on until dusk and banish the ghosts with rum."

- Hunter S. Thompson, *The Rum Diary*

Desperate Dick chased Nancy, Barb and Trix.

"Stay away!"
They screamed and pitched a fit.

He followed them around to no avail,
Till Dick passed out stiff,

like a **S**idepiece wearing tails.

➤◆ Sidepiece ◆➤

1 oz gin
1 oz pear vodka
1/2 oz elderflower liqueur
1/2 oz sloe gin
3/4 oz lime juice
1/4 oz simple syrup
Cucumber

Muddle cucumber in a mixer. Add liquors, juice, syrup and ice.
Shake and strain through mesh sieve into coupe glass.

"Sober or blotto, this is your motto:
Keep muddling through."

- P. G. Wodehouse, *A Damsel in Distress*

"Tequila I find makes all parties easier,"
Rude Ronald said to his friend Weezer.

"It has the potential to turn the cute ones from
teasers to pleasers."

Toronja Head Honcho

2 oz tequila
1 oz fresh squeezed grapefruit juice
1 oz fresh squeezed lemon juice
Q grapefruit soda
grapefruit zest

Combine liquor, juice and ice in empty shaker. Shake. Shake and strain into coupe and top off with grapefruit soda. Garnish with grapefruit zest.

"Sublime is something you choke on after a shot of tequila."

- Mark Z. Danielewski, *House of Leaves*

"**U**lterior Motive is far from the truth,"
Sly Mark said to Victoria Sleuth.

Leaning in to pour,
His eyes told the truth.

"Another drink my dear? It's only 10 proof."

Ulterior Motive

1 oz gin
1 oz Lillet Blanc
1/2 oz limoncello
1/2 oz Licor 43
1/2 oz dry curaçao
1 dash cranberry bitters
Lemon twist

Pour all the liquors over ice into a shaker. Stir. Strain into martini glass. Express and discard lemon twist.

"Men who call just to say hello generally
have ulterior motives."

- Stieg Larsson

"Vicious I'm not!"
Said Victor the snot.

"It's just that the **V**odka
Says things I would not."

➤◆ Vendetta ◆◀

2 oz tomato and black pepper vodka
1/2 oz Cynar
4 oz tomato juice
1/2 oz lime juice
1/4 oz soy sauce
4 dashes hot sauce

Combine all ingredients in a shaker over ice. Strain over ice into highball glass. Don't garnish. Just don't.

"Alcohol may be man's worst enemy,
but the Bible says love your enemy."

- Frank Sinatra

"**W**ine over time is simply divine,"
Brenda slurred to Dr. Stein.
"Perhaps, it may appear my dear,
But keep it from spinning in my beer!"

Wheel of Time

1 1/2 oz cognac
1 oz Malbec
3/4 oz sweet vermouth
3/4 oz lime juice
3/4 oz lemon juice

1/4 oz simple syrup
2 dashes angostura bitters
Egg white
Orange twist

Combine the liquors, juices, syrup, bitters and egg white in a shaker and dry shake. Add ice, shake and strain into a rocks glass with a big ice cube.

"I cook with wine, sometimes I even add it to the food."

- W.C. Fields

"I hate him!"
Proclaimed Olivia Sue.

"He's a cad!"
Chimed in her girlfriend Lu Lu.

"Although I've tried, he makes me blue."

Agreeing, Lu Lu nodded, "He's no Xanadu."

As Olivia slumped and turned to cry,
Her girlfriend Lu Lu caught his eye.

"Meet you at two?"
She mouthed with no sound,
"Same as last night, out on the grounds."

⟶◆ Xanadu ◆⟵

2 oz citra-citrus infused gin
1/2 oz campari
1 oz grapefruit juice
1/2 oz lemon juice
2 dashes orange bitters

2 oz grapefruit bitters
Egg white
2 oz tonic water
Lemon twist

Pour tonic in an empty rocks glass. Combine the liquors, juices, bitters and egg white in an empty shaker, dry shake. Add ice, shake and strain over the tonic. Express and discard lemon twist.

"I went out with a guy that once told me I didn't need to drink to make myself more fun to be around. I told him, I'm drinking so that you are more fun to be around."

- Chelesa Handler, *My Horizontal Life: A Collection of One Night Stands*

"An old toast that all should know!"
Said old man Tate, his wife in tow.

All gather round to enjoy the show,

As old man Tate toasts to Yellow snow.

—◆ Yellow Snow ◆—

1 oz Yellow Chartreuse
1/2 oz Galliano
1/2 oz Licor 43
1/2 oz limoncello
1/2 oz lemon juice
Crushed ice
Paper cone

Combine all the liquors and juice into shaker with ice. Shake and strain into cone.

"I drink to make other people more interesting."

- Ernest Hemingway

All of the guests so it's been said,
Flirted, drank and lost their heads.

"Imbibe, indulge, til noses turn red!"
Yelled the crocked Colonel Ted.

"Turn out the lights when they're done,"
His wife, to the maid said.

"I've had too many **Z**ombies and must go to bed!

Zombie Apocalypse

1 oz black rum
1 oz aged rum
½ oz Averna amaro
½ oz dry curaçao
½ oz velvet falernum
½ oz 151 proof rum

1 oz pineapple juice
1 oz passion fruit puree
½ oz lime juice
½ oz orgeat syrup
Mint

Combine all ingredients except mint and 151 proof rum into a shaker over ice. Shake and strain into a tiki cup. Gently float the 151 proof rum on top of the cocktail. Garnish with a sprig of mint.

"It had been a gay party and different stages
of sobriety were represented."

- F. Scott Fitzgerald, *This Side of Paradise*

Acknowledgments

First I would like to thank Nick Courtright and Kyle McCord at Atmosphere Press for believing in this manuscript and encouraging me to follow my dream of getting it published. I greatly appreciate Bryce Wilson whose counsel during the editorial stages was invaluable. I am also grateful to Ronaldo Alves's talent for bringing a sense of style and marketing around the book cover design.

I am immensely grateful to Randy Fair for his passionate interest in my book getting published and his personal introduction of Nick Courtright at Atmosphere Press. Randy's insight through his own publishing and marketing experience were invaluable, insightful, and encouraging.

Additionally, my special thanks to Glen Rogers for his enthusiastic belief and promotion of me and my book which led to the contacts of Randy Fair and the professionals at Atmosphere Press.

I want to acknowledge Mike Claypool, whose passion and creative flair for mixology contributed immensely to the recipes in this book.

Finally, I tip my hat with much love to both Danie and Chris Kinkade and Scott Bartolacci. Through their special friendship, I've shared my love for entertaining and cocktails, and they were truly the inspiration for this book.

About Atmosphere Press

Atmosphere Press is an independent, full-service publisher for excellent books in all genres and for all audiences. Learn more about what we do at atmospherepress.com.

We encourage you to check out some of Atmosphere's latest releases, which are available at Amazon.com and via order from your local bookstore:

Love and Asperger's: Jim and Mary's Excellent Adventure, by Mary A. Johnson, Ph.D.

Down, Looking Up, by Connie Rubsamen

Embodying the 12 Steps Workbook: Kundalini Yoga for Recovery, by Rachel Surinderjot Kaur

Home at the Office: Working Remotely as a Way of Life, by Barbori Garnet

God? WTF?!, by Charmaine Loverin

Chasing Corporate Compliance: Why Your Company is Playing Compliance Catch Up!, by John C. Vescera

My Way Forward: Turning Tragedy into Triumph, by Molei Wright

In Pursuit of Calm, by Daniel Fuselier, PsyD

UFOs of the Kickapoo, by John Sime

About the Author

Brian Crawford has had a long career in both Food & Beverage and Catering. As a person who loves entertaining in his 19th Century home, coupled with his passion for mixology, the birth of this book was a natural. Brian is an artist, author, life coach, Quantum Healer and Etiquette Coach currently living in the Florida Keys. There is much truth in the saying "write what you know.", Brian and his guests can relate to the situations induced by the imbibing in the story line in this book. Cheers!

"Natives of the Florida Keys often refer to themselves as Conchs, and for good reason: They have been drinking."

- Dave Barry, *Best. State. Ever.:*
A Florida Man Defends His Homeland

9 781639 882243